Nottingl
Lost Lan(

C000072449

on old picture postcards

David Ottewell

1. A superb photographic card from the 1920s, published by Spree, and featuring three trams outside Victoria Station on Mansfield Road.

**Printed by
Adlard Print and Typesetting Services,
Ruddington, Notts.**

2. **Queen Victoria's** statue was unveiled in July 1905. This postcard by Panzi & Co. shows the large crowd at the event. *(see illus. 13).*

3. A Boots postcard featuring both the Exchange and Victoria's statue, putting both in-to perspective in the Market Place, then covered with outdoor stalls, and the largest market square in England, covering 5½ acres. The Exchange, demolished in 1926, also housed meetings on council business and various exhibitions and concerts took place. The card was posted at Jacksdale in July 1914.

Designed and published by Reflections of a Bygone Age,
Keyworth, Nottingham 1992
*Reprinted 1994, 1995, 1996 (twice), 1998, 1999,
2000 and 2002*

ISBN 0 946245 52 5

INTRODUCTION

The first picture postcard in Great Britain was published in 1894. Initially, until 1902, the Post Office only allowed the address to be written on the reverse of the card with any message, strictly limited in length, being placed with the picture on the front. However, in 1902, rules were relaxed so that a more substantial message could be included alongside the address on the rear of the card. This contributed to a boom in postcard production and useage to such an extent that at its height in the first decade of the twentieth century there were upwards of 3 million cards being posted daily. The so-called 'Golden Age' of postcards continued until the First World War and even after this time large numbers of cards continued to be sent.

It is from this wealth of material, real photographic, printed or artist-drawn, that the illustrations in this book have been chosen. Most areas had their own postcard publishers and Nottingham was no exception with such names as C & A.G. Lewis, Peveril, Henson and Co., Boots and Albert Hindley's "Clumber" series to the fore. These, along with National publishers such as Wrench, Raphael Tuck and Valentines of Dundee provide both the postcard collector and the person interested in local history with many hundreds of different images of Nottingham as it has developed in the twentieth century.

Nottingham has changed in many respects over the last ninety years and, in spite of the valiant efforts of concerned individuals and groups such as the Civic Society, not always for the better. The postcards and the accompanying captions stir memories of this period: of buildings long gone, such as the Exchange and the Black Boy; of buildings fallen into disuse like the Bluecoat Schools, of landmarks such as the Victoria Statue — removed to its less prominent site on the Embankment, and of atmospheres like that generated by the Old Central Market, which once experienced was never forgotten. Take a postcard trip down memory lane.

David Ottewell, March 1992.

Front cover: **The Exchange** dominated the Market Place for two hundred years from its erection in 1726. It contained various shops and businesses, including over sixty butchers' stalls in an area known as the Shambles. Postcard by C. & A.G. Lewis, posted at Louth in January 1917. Adverts on the blinds in front of the Exchange include Beecroft & Sons (toys, games, useful presents) and Stapleton & Son (cash drapers).

4. Nottingham publishers C. & A.G. Lewis published this card of one of the top fairground attractions of **Goose Fair** when it was held in the Market Place. By the twentieth century the fair was predominantly for entertainment only rather than a provisions event. Market Place redevelopment saw the fair move to the Forest site in the late 1920s.

GOOSE FAIR, NOTTINGHAM.

5. A more panoramic view of **Goose Fair** on a Peveril Real Photo Series postcard no. 243, published about 1908. The last fair held here was in 1927.

6. The 'Mikado Cafe' on Long Row was a popular meeting place for the people of Nottingham from the late Victorian era until the early 1960s. Shops to the right of it were the London Goldsmiths, Edwin Harris & Co., A.D. Robertson, and J. Lyons & Co. Ltd., (another famous cafe). Postcard by Henson & Co. of Pelham Street was published in June 1911 and shows part of the celebrations and procession for George V's coronation.

7. The 'Kirkewhite Tavern' in Cheapside was named after the poet Henry Kirkewhite, who was born in the inn above his father's butchers shop.

8. The 'Black Boy Hotel' on the right of this 1960s postcard was designed by Watson Fothergill, the famous Nottingham architect, in 1887. Shamefully, it was demolished to make way for shops.

9. The obelisk at the junction of King Street and Queen Street was 25 feet high and carved out of red granite. It stood as a memorial to Boer War victims from the Nottingham and Notts volunteer battalions. Road access needs saw it moved to its present site on the Forest. The postcard was by A. & G. Taylor of London and posted from Nottingham in October 1906.

10. Skinner and Rook's shop was a prominent landmark at the junction of Long Row and Clumber Street. Its fame resulted in a price of a quarter of a million pounds being paid for it in 1955 when it was redeveloped. The white doorway in the centre background belonged to the 'Kardomah Cafe' referred to by the writer of the postcard as the place where she works. C. & A.G. Lewis card no.27.

PELHAM STREET, NOTTINGHAM.

11. This view looking up **Pelham Street** from Long Row reveals many changes. The old Boots shop on the right is fondly remembered by many people: the building remains, but its inside — where it gained most of its charm — has been sadly gutted. On the left, the premises now house the Alliance and Leicester Building Society. Peveril Real Photo series no. 221.

12. 'Ye Olde Talbot' on Long Row dated from Elizabethan times: it was knocked down to make way for the modern 'Talbot'. Interestingly, during demolition a vault was uncovered containing the body of a soldier and his horse, a mystery which remains unsolved to this day. Peveril series no. 564.

13. **Queen Victoria's statue** was built in marble by Albert Toft on the edge of the Market Place to commemorate the reign. It was unveiled by the Duchess of Portland on 28th July 1905, and stood for 48 years until road widening necessitated its removal to the Embankment. In the centre background is Pearson Brothers shop, a prominent feature of Long Row for many years until it was closed in 1989 and the rear removed. At present all that remains is the facade, which is in a dangerous condition. Card posted at Beeston in March 1915.

DERBY ROAD, NOTTINGHAM

14. **The Albert Hotel** stood on Derby Road until it was demolished in 1970 to make way for the inner ring road. It had a chequered history, surviving an explosion in 1911, and being extended with a new wing and Scotch bar in the 1930s. Postcard by Boots Cash Chemists, posted from Nottingham in September 1916.

HENSON & CO., PHOTOGRAPHERS·
ALBERT HALL, NOTTINGHAM
(Destroyed by Fire April 22nd, 1906.   This Photo was taken April 18th, 1906.

15. Watson Fothergill designed the original **Albert Hall**, opened by the mayor, John Manning, in 1876. In 1902 it became known as the Albert Hall Methodist Mission. Local photographers Henson & Co. took this picture four days before a fire destroyed the building in April 1906. Postcard by Sheppard & Co., Nottingham.

16. The new Drill Hall on Derby Road was opened in February 1912 by Sir John French, who was to take a leading part in the First World War. It lasted only 23 years before fire destroyed it in November 1935. "Rex" series postcard no. 256, posted at Boston in October 1925. *"Goose Fair was attended by thousands of people. It was a wonder I did not get lost,"* wrote the sender of the card.

17. From 1798 to 1926 the impressive building seen here stood where the Robin Hood Statue is now found, to the left of the Castle Gateway. Initially used as a riding school by the Nottingham troop of Yeomanry cavalry, it later became a drill hall for the Robin Hood Rifles. This card was published anonymously in 1921.

18. This 1906 card by Valentine of Dundee features **'The Gate Hangs Well'**, originally known as the 'Hanging Gate'. Its landlord in 1900 was Nathan Woodward, and the inn was one of two in Brewhouse Yard at the time, the other being 'The Trip to Jerusalem'. The 'Gate' had been demolished by the start of the First World War.

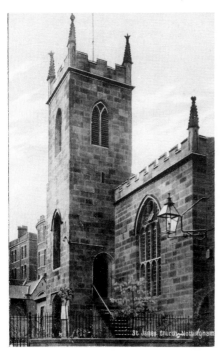

19. St. James Church on Standard Hill opened in 1808 on land provided by the Duke of Newcastle, because it had been decided that Nottingham needed a fourth large church. It lasted until 1936, when it was demolished: a nurses' home was built on the site. "Clumber" series postcard no. 234, published by Albert Hindley.

FIRST COTTON MILL in the World,   No 547
WOLLATON STREET, NOTTINGHAM

20. There was great rivalry between Arkwright and Hargreaves to set up cotton mills and both established one in Nottingham in the 1760s. Arkwright's was called Hockley Mill and was situated in Goose Gate. James Hargreaves sited his on Wollaton Street, where a plaque on the wall claimed it was the *'first cotton mill in the world'*. The postcard was published by W.H. Smith & Son.

21. The 'Royal Hippodrome' at the end of Wollaton Street was opened in 1908 as a variety theatre and was one of the largest in the country. This probably contributed to its downfall, for with the waning of interest in variety in the 1920s it became harder to fill and run at a profit. Postcard by Baker & Co. of Nottingham, sent to Lincoln in July 1909.

22. In the 1920s the modern phenomenon of talking pictures was considered a much more profitable venture than variety theatre; a screen was fitted in the old 'Hippodrome' building and it was renamed the 'Gaumont Cinema', running until 1971. The building was demolished two years later. Also featured on this c.1952 card are the 'County Hotel' (right) and the Automobile Association offices.

23. This statue was erected in memory of **Samuel Morley,** the local M.P., in 1888. Its position in the middle of the road outside the 'Theatre Royal' meant that it became a hindrance to traffic: in 1926 it was decided to resite it at the Arboretum. Unfortunately, the statue was badly damaged in the process and a new bust had to be made as a replacement. Real photographic card by S.S., no.45 in a series.

24. The Nottingham 'Empire' (on the right of this c.1908 "Woodbury" series postcard by Eyre and Spottiswoode) opened in 1908 and over the years attracted many of the music hall greats. Little Tich, George Robey, Gracie Fields, W.C. Fields and Max Miller all appeared there. The decline of music hall led to falling audiences, resulting in the Empire's closure in 1958.

25. This "Clumber" series card (no.134) dating from 1906 shows Milton Street from its junction with Parliament Street. The building on the extreme right was the 'Milton's Head Hotel', which along with other buildings on this side of the road was sold for demolition in 1969 and is now part of the Victoria Centre. The tram standards are also a feature of the scene.

MILTON STRE

26. This view is looking the opposite way along Milto
Clumber and Parliament Streets. This landmark was
horror the changes that are taking place. Among th
Testing Rooms'. The tram is en route from Market
tingham in October 1912.

NOTTINGHAM

...nd features the 'Old Corner Pin' pub on the corner of
...0 for redevelopment and many of us are watching in
...s on the left — all demolished — is 'Bain's Eyesight
...Sherwood. "Peveril" series card, posted from Not-

27. Holy Trinity Church, with its 177-foot spire, was built in 1841 and soon had the largest congregation in Nottingham. Its spire became unsafe and had to be removed in 1942. The church itself lasted into the 1950s before being replaced by Trinity Square Car Park which opened in 1964. "Clumber" series card no. 146, postally used in 1908.

VICTORIA STATION, NOTTINGHAM

28. The Great Central Railway's **Victoria Station** was built at a cost of over a million pounds and was opened in 1900. 67 years later it was closed as part of a rationalisation programme, and all the station facade — except the clocktower — was demolished. W. H. Smith's "Kingsway" series postcard.

INTERIOR, VICTORIA STATION, NOTTINGHAM

29. "Peveril" series card showing two of the twelve platforms in Victoria Station. It covered a vast area, and a large number of homes and other buildings were cleared to make way for it. The Victoria Centre shopping complex/car park has replaced the station.

30. The Old Mechanics Institute was demolished in 1964, but it had an illustrious history: it was the site of the first electric light in Nottingham, and hosted lectures from personalities such as Charles Dickens, Captain Scott, Conan Doyle and Oscar Wilde. As well as being a place of education, it housed the Mechanics Picture Cinema. "Peveril" series card no. 2027, posted from Nottingham in March 1913.

31. The imposing **Wesleyan Chapel** on Mansfield Road was opened in 1874. It had a varied life, housing Christian Scientists and Assemblies of God before seeing its last service in May 1973.

THE NOTTINGHAM HOSPITAL FOR WOMEN

32. Aerial view of **Peel Street Hospital** (built in 1929 at a cost of £47,600) published by Aerofilms. It was soon extended and as late as 1975 a new central labour suite was built, costing a quarter of a million pounds. Despite this updating and a lot of good feeling towards the hospital, it still fell prey to 'rationalisation' and closed in 1981.

Grand Theatre, NOTTINGHAM.

33. The Grand Theatre on Hyson Green had many uses — theatre, music hall and opera. Charlie Chaplin appeared here in 1904. In 1926 it was turned into the Granda Cinema, and for the next thirty years entertained people on the silver screen. "Clumber" series card no. 163.

34. Bluecoat School, designed by T.C. Hine, was opened in 1853. A notable feature was the two statues of pupils in school uniform — one can be seen on this "Clumber" card no. 150, sent to Holt, Norfolk, in March 1907. The school moved to larger premises on Aspley Lane in 1967, whilst the building remains by the International Community Centre on Mansfield Road.

35. Many still mourn the passing of the **Central Market,** seen here on a "Rex" series card no. 1858. It opened in November 1928 to take the stalls ejected from the Market Place during its modernisation. A unique atmosphere developed at the location between Parliament Street, King Edward Street and Huntingdon Street, until it moved in 1972 to its present home in the Victoria Centre.

36. Completed in 1860, the old **Nottingham prison** was situated where King Edward Street meets Parliament Street. It soon proved to be too small, though, and in 1891 prisoners were transferred to a new jail at Bagthorpe. The writer of this card, posted to Eastbourne in January 1913, says: *"Have been in Nottingham over a month now ... there's heaps to see in a town like this. My postcard is rather a dreary one .. but better next time."*

37. The Palais De Danse. The building in this view is still in existence, but has had a varied history since its opening in April 1925. The globe on the roof, much commented upon in the past, has now gone, along with the passing tram (on route 4 to Basford). Local publisher Spree produced this postcard (no.971), sent to New Ollerton in November 1929. The building now houses Ritzy's nightclub.

Spree.

38. Sneinton Hermitage on a "Peveril" series card no. 574. For many years, caves were used in and around Nottingham as dwellings, workplaces and storerooms. The Great Northern Railway began to remove Sneinton Hermitage in 1897, and the final caves made way for road widening in 1904. The postcard was sent to Aberystwyth in August 1913.

ST. ANN'S CHURCH, NOTTINGHAM

39. St. Ann's Church, a prominent local landmark for over a hundred years is shown on this "Peveril" series postcard no. 103. Although it was demolished in 1971, it is still remembered fondly by many people.

TRAM TERMINUS, ST. ANNS WELL ROAD, NOTTINGHAM.

40. St. Anns Well Road Tram Terminus, with a no.6 tram (St. Anns Well — Lenton — Radford) in view. In the background can be seen a horse trough and drinking fountain on the site of the old rag well. W.H. Smith postcard no. 217, sent to Chatsworth Avenue in Nottingham from Jackson Street in January 1914.

St. Peter's Square, Nottingham.

41. The General Post Office, Albert Street, is now where Marks and Spencers stands, but opened in 1848 to deal with the upsurge of mail after the introduction of the penny post in 1840. However, the increase in mail soon exceeded the capacity of the office to deal with it, and larger premises had to be found. On the left of this c.1908 "Peveril" series card can be seen the awning of J.G. Gant, shirt and collar maker.

WALTER FOUNTAIN, LISTER GATE, NOTTINGHAM.

42. The Walter Fountain was erected by the son of John Walter M.P. in his memory after the latter's death in 1847. It consisted of a 50-foot tower with four drinking fountains, each topped by a medallion portrait of John Walter. This view looking up Lister Gate also shows on the extreme left 'The Sawyers Arms', while further up is the Caledonian Hotel. In the centre background are the premises of Clarke, Dentist. "Peveril" series card no. 207.

43. "Peveril" series card sent from Nottingham to Ireland in 1924 shows the Walter Fountain and Lucky Corner. The railings on the right belong to the old Collins almshouses. The Fountain itself was removed for road widening in 1950.

44. Woolworth's store on Lister Gate was a popular location for Nottingham shoppers for many years, but was closed in the late 1980s. This card by Valentine of Dundee dates from the 1950s.

45. Narrow Marsh was one of the notorious slum areas of the city, with a rabbit warren of alleys, courts and yards. In an effort to clean up its image, the corporation tried to rename the area Red Lion Street after a local public house. This superficial beautification, though, had little effect and the area began to be flattened in the 1930s. On this "Clumber" series postcard, the 'Old Star & Garter' is on the left.

46. A farmhouse in **Kirkes Yard** in Narrow Marsh, dating from the fifteenth century, and a relic of earlier days when the area had more open spaces. W.H. Smith postcard.

SHIRE HALL, NOTTINGHAM   No 550

47. Not quite a lost landmark, but after a long and sometimes painful history of dispensing justice, the **Shire Hall** was finally closed in the 1980s and sold to a private company. Many people are now watching anxiously to see the fate of this small piece of Nottingham's heritage. Postcard by W.H. Smith.

48. The James Store, one of the most popular shops on Carrington Street, a widely frequented shopping street until the Broad Marsh centre truncated it. "Peveril" series postcard no. 3052, sent to Scarborough in August 1913.

49. For many years **Arkwright Street** was a thriving thoroughfare with many specialist shops. The large car, for instance, is parked outside Tom Sanderson's tripe shop, while to the left are the premises of T.B. Whitby and Stray. The bridge in the background formed part of the extensive Nottingham viaduct taking trains into Victoria Station on the Great Central line. Card published by C. & A.G. Lewis.

50. **St. Gabriel's Mission** was a corrugated iron building on the corner of Bathley Street and Lamcote Grove in the Meadows. It was built at the turn of the century by the Smith banking family as a private mission. Attached to St. Saviours Parish, it was run by the Church Pastoral Aid Society. Closure came in 1954. "C.A." series postcard.

51. As this "Rex" series card no. 1873 shows, it was difficult to miss the **'Globe'** cinema when travelling from Trent Bridge into Nottingham. It opened in 1912 to show films, which it continued to do — apart from a brief flirtation with bingo — until it closed in June 1962.